RATINGS' BADGES

GUNNERY

RADAR PLOT

TORPEDO
ANTI-SUBMARINE

RECORDER

PHYSICAL TRAINING

DIVING

NAVIGATOR'S
YEOMAN

MASTER-AT-ARMS

COMMUNICATIONS
(Captain's Yeoman)

COMMUNICATIONS

WEAPON
MECHANICIAN

ENGINEERING
MECHANIC

ENGINEERING
MECHANICIAN

ELECTRICAL

ELECTRICAL
MECHANICIAN

NAVAL AIRMAN
NAVAL AIR MECHANIC

AIRCRAFT
MECHANICIAN

PHOTOGRAPHER

MEDICAL ASSISTANT
MEDICAL TECHNICIAN

REGULATING

SUPPLY AND
SECRETARIAT

P. O. COXSWAIN

C.P.O. COXSWAIN

RATING AIRCREW

NAVAL PATROL ARMLET

BUGLER

GOOD SHOOTING

GOOD CONDUCT (12 years)

Series 606B

This carefully planned reference book will help to answer many of the questions that children ask.

Interesting and accurate information about the Navy is given within the limits of a relatively simple vocabulary. Even children whose reading experience is limited will be encouraged to find out for themselves by the excellent full-colour illustrations and clear text, thus gaining extra reading practice.

'People at work'
THE SAILOR

by I. & J. HAVENHAND
with illustrations by JOHN BERRY

Publishers: Ladybird Books Ltd . Loughborough
ⓒ Ladybird Books Ltd (formerly Wills & Hepworth Ltd) 1967
Printed in England

THE SAILOR

Before the year 1485 the kings of England had a navy only when they were at war. They hired cargo ships, like the one in the picture, from ship owners and had guns put on them. When the wars ended the guns were taken off and the ships were again used to carry goods.

In 1485 King Henry VII started a full-time navy. He started it with two ships. These ships always had guns on them and the sailors were the King's Men.

7214 0071 X

To-day, ships of the Navy are still the Queen's Ships and the sailors who man them are the Queen's Men. A sailor has the name of his ship on his hat band. In front of the name of the ship are the letters H.M.S. These letters stand for Her Majesty's Ship.

All men who become sailors in the Navy have to pass medical tests. They have also to be able to learn how to do the special kinds of work needed in modern fighting ships. Before they learn this, all sailors are trained in seamanship.

Training in seamanship helps sailors to know all about ships and the sea. The training also helps the sailors to learn to live together and keep a ship safe and seaworthy.

The sailors learn how to handle ropes and anchors. They learn how to use small boats and how to save lives. All sailors must be able to swim at least two lengths of a swimming bath. They have to do this with their clothes on.

After training in seamanship many sailors join the Seaman Branch of the Navy.

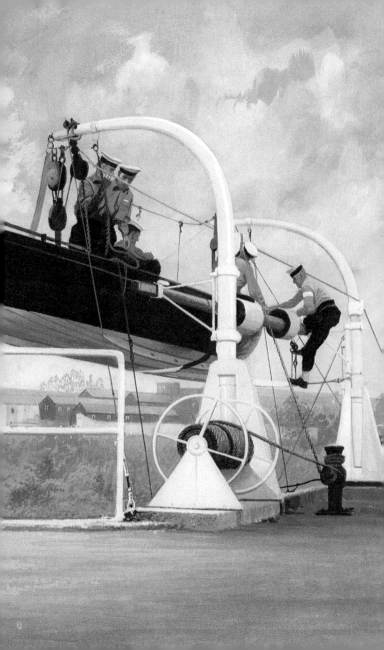

Most men of the Seaman Branch work with the weapons on ships. They may train as gun crews and work in the turrets of the large guns.

To-day, the ships which carry the largest guns are cruisers. Some cruisers have guns which fire six-inch shells and some that fire three-inch shells.

Cruisers are now made to carry helicopters on special decks aft (at the back). The most modern cruisers are H.M.S. Tiger, H.M.S. Lion and H.M.S. Blake. Each of these cruisers carries seven-hundred and fifty men.

Enemy aeroplanes and submarines are the biggest dangers to warships. Men on the ships use radar to spot aeroplanes before they would otherwise be seen.

Radar works by using wireless waves which are sent out from the ship. If they hit anything, the wireless waves bounce back. When they bounce back, they make spots of light on a screen which is like a television screen. Men on the ships watch the radar screens all the time. The men can work out how far away and in what direction the aeroplanes are flying.

Modern fighting ships carry guided missiles as well as guns. Guided missiles are special kinds of rockets. On warships, guided missiles are for use against enemy aeroplanes. The missiles may be fired before the planes can be seen. Seamen, using radar and radio signals, 'fix' the missiles on their targets. When the missiles hit the targets they explode.

Guided missiles called 'Seacats' are carried on frigates. 'Seacat' is a short range missile. Destroyers carry 'Seacat' and 'Seaslug' missiles. 'Seaslug' missiles are medium range missiles and can travel further than 'Seacat' missiles.

Destroyers, which are larger than frigates, are very fast ships. The newest destroyers have boosters for their engines to make them still faster.

On the newest destroyers four-hundred and fifty men live and work. As well as 'Seaslug' and 'Seacat' guided missiles, destroyers carry large guns. Some of them carry anti-submarine mortars as well.

The newest destroyers carry helicopters for anti-submarine work. Each helicopter can carry a homing torpedo. A torpedo is a special kind of bomb with a motor in it. Homing torpedoes find enemy submarines and then explode.

On all ships there are sailors who listen for enemy submarines. The sailors listen for any strange sounds from under the sea. Even little sounds can be picked up by the special kinds of microphones in the ships. These sounds are heard by sailors wearing ear-phones.

If the sailors think the sound comes from an enemy submarine they give the alarm. The ship's captain tries to make his ship safe from attack by the submarine and starts to hunt for it. He signals to other ships asking them to help find the submarine.

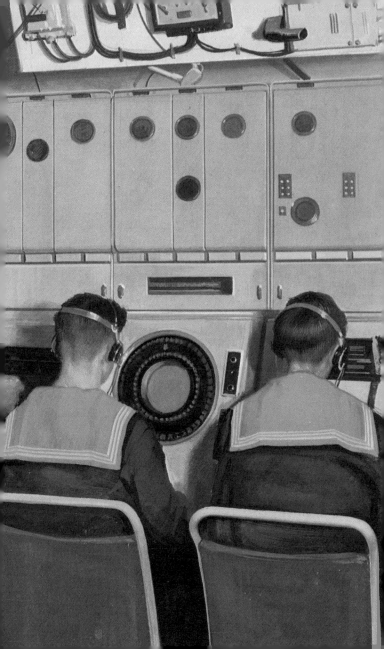

Frigates are ships which are made to hunt and destroy enemy submarines.

Some sailors on frigates work in the 'Sonar' Control Room. In this room they use powerful listening sets which help to tell them exactly where the submarines are. They can tell if the submarines change course or slow down or even if torpedoes are fired at their ship.

When the position of a submarine is fixed, the 'Sonar' Controller fires the anti-submarine mortars. These are like bombs and they are set to explode under the sea near the submarine.

Some sailors ask specially to serve on submarines. They must pass tests to show that they are very fit and are able to live and work on these under-sea warships. About eighty men live together for many weeks in very little space.

The newest submarines have nuclear (or atom) powered engines and can stay under the sea for months. Sometimes submarines hunt each other.

Targets on land can be attacked by some submarines. These carry sixteen 'Polaris' missiles. 'Polaris' missiles can be fired from under the sea and have atomic war-heads.

Aircraft carriers are the biggest warships. About one thousand, five hundred sailors live on an aircraft carrier. As well as the sailors, there are men of the Fleet Air Arm.

An aircraft carrier is a floating air-base. It can move aircraft thousands of miles to within striking distance of an enemy.

The aircraft have folding wings which take up less space and allow more planes to be carried.

Some of the planes are stored below the flight deck and are carried up and down in large lifts.

On the flight deck of an aircraft carrier the men wear brightly coloured jackets. Each colour is for a different kind of work.

A steam driven catapult is used to give the aircraft more speed for taking off.

Naval aircraft are very fast and land at high speed. When they touch down on the flight deck they have to be stopped quickly. A hook underneath the aircraft hooks on to an arrester wire which stretches across the deck.

When aircraft are taking off and landing there is always a helicopter flying close to the aircraft carrier in case of accidents.

At times, the Navy and the Army have to work together. Special ships called 'Assault' Ships are used to carry soldiers and the tanks and guns they need. When they have to leave assault ships, the soldiers and tanks are put into landing craft. The landing craft, which are in the holds of the ships, are used for carrying loads to the beaches.

The sterns of assault ships are like huge doors. When these doors are opened, water comes into the holds of the ships. The landing craft float and sail out, carrying tanks, soldiers and supplies.

Sailors on small ships, called minesweepers, find mines and destroy them. Mines are kinds of bombs that are put into the sea to sink ships.

Some mines explode if ships touch them. Other mines are magnetic and these are attracted towards ships, because the ships are made of steel. 'Acoustic' mines are made to explode by the sound of a ship's engines and propellers as they pass over them.

Minesweepers are made mostly of wood and aluminium and the sailors must not take iron or steel things on board with them.

When the sailors are sweeping for magnetic mines, they let out a thick loop of electric cable. This is towed behind the ship. A powerful electric current is passed through the cable and this explodes magnetic mines that are near.

To destroy acoustic mines, the sailors use a different sweep. They use an acoustic hammer. This is a machine which is towed behind the minesweeper. It makes a noise like a large ship and this explodes the mines.

When a passage has been cleared of mines, the sailors mark it with buoys.

Sometimes fighting ships have to stay at sea for a long time. All the things the sailors and ships need are taken to them. Special ships called Fleet Support Ships are used to do this.

Some of these ships are floating workshops. The sailors in them are able to mend ships that have broken down or have been damaged.

Other fleet support ships act as 'mother' ships to destroyers, submarines or minesweepers. The sailors from the smaller ships can go on board the mother ship when their ship is being refitted or repaired.

Sailors of the Royal Fleet Auxiliary take stores and ammunition to naval ships. These sailors belong to the Merchant Navy and not to the Royal Navy.

Most ships use fuel oil to drive their engines. Sailors in the Royal Fleet Auxiliary make sure that the naval ships always have plenty of fuel oil.

The captains of the ships arrange a meeting place at sea. When they meet, a rope is fired by rocket from the tanker to the naval ship. This is used to pull fuel pipes across. The ships sail along as the fuel oil flows from one to the other.

All ships in the Navy, except the smaller minesweepers, carry sailors who have been trained as divers. These sailors have asked to do this kind of work and have been specially trained.

The divers inspect the under-water parts of ships to see that no mines have been fastened to them by enemy divers.

Any repairs that have to be done under the water are carried out by the divers. Ships' divers are called frogmen. They wear special suits and have flippers on their feet. The divers carry their own supply of air.

Sometimes divers have to jump from helicopters. They do this to reach aircraft that have crashed into the sea.

There are some specially trained divers called Clearance Divers. Clearance divers have the longest training of all naval divers. They can dive deeper and stay under water for a longer time than other divers. At times they wear special observation suits which allow them to go very deep indeed.

Clearance divers are based in this country and they are flown to anywhere in the world when they are needed.

Sailors on the ice patrol ship H.M.S. Protector spend most of the year in the Antarctic.

Because of the ice, extra thick plates have been put on the ship round the water line. The inside of the ship is specially lined to keep out the cold.

H.M.S. Protector is used to carry stores to men at bases on the Antarctic Ice Cap. Two helicopters are used to help carry stores from the ship.

Captains of all ships need good maps of the oceans and seas. These maps are called charts.

The Navy has sailors, in special ships called Survey Ships, who keep the charts up to date. The sailors find out where there are sandbanks, rocks, sunken ships or anything that may be a danger to other ships.

The charts that our sailors make are so good that they are used by ships of other countries. Sailors in the Navy first started charting the oceans more than two hundred years ago.

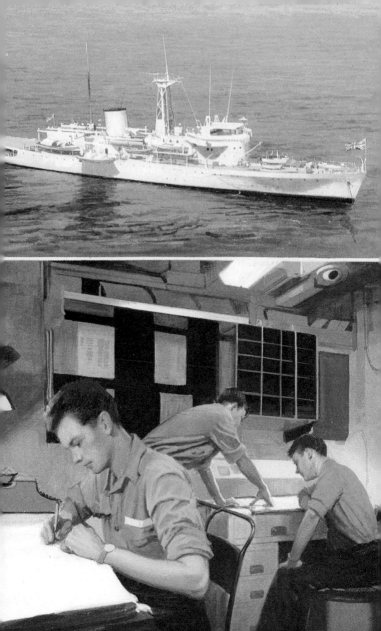

Some sailors in the Navy serve on ships that are quite small. These are fast patrol boats that can travel at about fifty miles an hour. The boats are often used in coastal and shallow waters. The ships carry anti-submarine torpedoes but these can be changed for guns if the ships have to be used in large rivers.

Sailors on other kinds of small boats are like sentries. They look out and listen for very small submarines that are used to attack big ships in harbours.

On all ships of the Navy, sailors work spells of duty called 'watches'. They all do four hours on duty and then have four hours off. This goes on all day and all night.

The ships have to be ready for action at all times, and there is always a 'look-out' on duty. Every day the guns are cleaned and radar, radio and electrical parts are tested.

Some sailors clean the mess decks. These are the parts of ships where the sailors live. The officers on duty inspect the ships twice a day to make sure that the ships are kept clean and tidy.

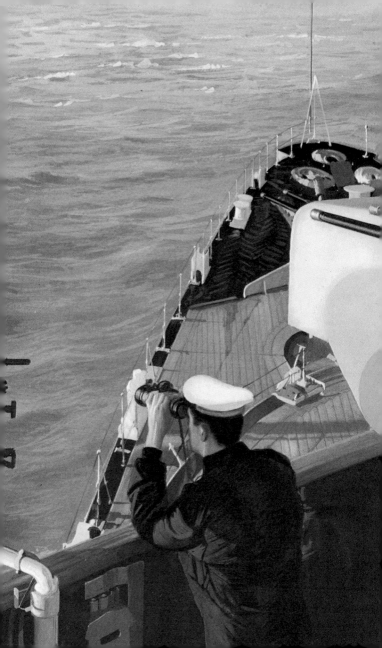

There is not much living space for sailors on the mess decks. They have to keep all their belongings, eat their meals and sleep there.

Many sailors sleep in hammocks. Hammocks are made of strips of canvas and ropes. These are tied to hooks and stretched across the mess decks.

The ship's captain and officers sleep in cabins.

Sailors are proud to belong to the Royal Navy. They enjoy working together and make many friends. They like being on board ship and look forward to visiting different parts of the world.